Piano Music for One Hand

A COLLECTION OF STUDIES, EXERCISES AND PIECES

Selected and Edited with Prefatory Notes by RAYMOND LEWENTHAL

ED-2773

ISBN 0-7935-5268-0

G. SCHIRMER, Inc.

DISTRIBUTED BY

HAL•LEONARD®
CORPORATION

7777 W. BLUEMOUND RD. P.O. BOX 13819 MILWAUKEE, WI 53213

PREFACE

At one time or another, most piano students have injured a hand through accident (usually baseball) or over-practice (rare!) thus providing themselves with a perfect excuse to stop practicing altogether while the ailing hand is pampered — *unless the wary and wise teacher has material on tap to occupy the healthy remaining hand.* This collection of one-hand pieces will prove most efficacious in stopping the fleeing arm-in-a-sling student dead in his tracks. It also, of course, can provide solace for music-loving persons who are permanently left with the use of only one hand.

Actually, however, the main purpose of this collection is to provide *left-hand* music for pianists who do not have any such temporary or permanent handicaps. The question that immediately arises is: "Why should someone with two perfectly good hands practice and play compositions for one hand?" The answer is that most people do *not* have two perfectly good hands. Their left hands are often very under-developed — rudimentary is a less euphonious but more truthful adjective. It is not uncommon to find pianists with quite fluent right hands, whose playing is marred by sluggish, slothful, inaccurate, unrhythmical left hands. In fact, every honest pianist has, at one time or another (or many times), come to the conclusion that his left hand needs special attention. A further question might be: "Why could not such pianists simply use two-hand piano music which has a difficult left-hand part to develop that hand?" Answer: one of the surest ways to develop left-hand technique is by playing pieces written for it *alone,* because they allow complete scrutiny of the left hand uncamouflaged by right-hand activity — putting the left hand under a microscope, so to speak.

Another likely benefit to be derived from playing left-hand pieces is an increase in sight-reading ability — for one of the problems in sight-reading is a cumbersome, inadequate left hand which cannot quickly grasp chords, leaps, and passages, and instantly find a usable fingering.

I cannot recommend too strongly that every piano student study at least one left-hand piece *each season* (and perform it frequently) no matter at what grade of technical proficiency he may have arrived. To this end, the compositions included in this collection extend over the entire range from very easy to very difficult. And the fact should not be overlooked that left-hand pieces make extremely effective peaks in recitals either as encores or on the printed program.

Some people are bound to accuse you of exhibitionism for playing left-hand pieces. The great pianist, Ignaz Friedman, played the Chopin etudes magnificently. When someone asked him why he played them so fast he said: "Because I can." If anyone asks *you* why you play left-hand pieces, you should answer: "Because I can" (make sure you *can*) and, indeed, there's a wide enough selection of pieces in this collection, at all grade levels, for you to choose works that can be within your possibilities after some sincere perspiration. The advantages to be gained from playing left-hand pieces in respect to general finger dexterity, control of the pedals, knowledge of fingering combinations and dynamic independence of fingers in balancing several voices in one hand, are immense. An articulate left hand has to be the foundation of every real piano technique. The left hand, as Chopin said, is the conductor. It supplies the rhythmic and harmonic base (as well as bass) of the musical structure. *Nota bene:* by "developed hand" I do not mean a loud, thumpy one. Quite the contrary. The player whose left hand thumps is usually trying to compensate for lack of agility by aggressive loudness (about this, more below).

The right hand, because it is used more frequently than the left by most people, is more subject to injury. This is one reason why perhaps 99% of all one-hand piano pieces is for left hand. Another is that the left hand is more readily adaptable for one-hand piano playing because the strongest part of the hand commands the upper (and usually melodic) parts of chords, and the strongest fingers usually play the strongest (highest) notes of the melody. Godowsky, one of the prime contributors to the left-hand literature, felt, also, that the left hand is more susceptible to development just because it is less used in daily life and, therefore, less cramped from writing, etc. Although most of the pieces in this collection are for left hand (as are, therefore, most of my comments), *they would be beneficial for, and adaptable to, the right hand.* (See comments below.)

Collecting left-hand music has long been one of my hobbies, a hobby which grew out of my deep interest in the possibilities of the piano and the pianist's fingers. It also grew out of my interest in pedagogical matters; and since I am my own prize pupil, you can believe me when I say it has been carried on with loving care. The more I indulged myself in this fascinating hobby, the more amazed I became at how much left-hand music has been written, and also—considering the quantity—how little of it is known even to knowledgeable professional pianists. For all but a few, left-hand music begins with the *Nocturne* by Scriabin (even his other left-hand piece, the *Prelude,* is much less known) and ends with Ravel's *Piano Concerto for Left Hand.* The intrinsic musical value of the left-hand repertoire varies widely. My aim here has been to select from my very large left-hand library utilitarian pieces which can also be said to have musical value as well. Most of the great composers have stayed away from one-hand music, although Ravel has proven what a master can do with the medium. And Sir Donald Francis Tovey — that great and profound savant — a man not given to gimmicks and passing fancies, considered that writing for the left hand was of great aesthetic interest because "the restrictions it imposes on the composer are a stimulus to his invention."

A BRIEF SURVEY OF ONE-HAND REPERTOIRE

One-hand keyboard music was very uncommon in the contrapuntal era. Composers of those days tried to use all possible members rather than eliminating some. It is said that Bach, while playing the violin, sometimes accompanied himself with his feet on the pedal-board of the organ! The earliest one-hand piece that I have found up to now is the little piece in A by C.P.E. Bach.

Italy is not a country one ordinarily associates with the cultivation of piano virtuosity. It has produced fewer great pianists than most of the other European countries; nor has the music written for the piano by Italian composers been, for the most part, noteworthy. Therefore, it is more than surprising to find that some of the earliest writers of left-hand music were Italian. In fact, *la mano sinistra* seems to have enjoyed quite a vogue in Italy during the first half of the last century. Pollini, Fumagalli, and Döhler (Italian born and died, despite the name) kept their right hands busy writing left-hand music (or perhaps they were left-handed!). The most prolific left-hand composer before Leopold Godowsky was Italian. His name was Bonamici, not to be confused with Buonamici. His three volumes of left-hand exercises and studies totaling some 200 pages are full of fascinating ideas.

Kalkbrenner, a pianist whom Chopin admired and with whom he almost decided to study, was famous for the equal development of both hands. He wrote a sonata, which many people, who have not taken the trouble to look it up, list as being for the left hand alone. In point of fact, it is *pour la main gauche principale*. In other words for two hands, with a difficult left-hand part. The short fugue included here *is* for left hand alone.

The great Czech virtuoso, Alexander Dreyschock, was famous for his left-hand technique. One of his specialties was playing the left-hand part of the *Revolutionary Etude* of Chopin *in octaves*. He also wrote several pieces for the left hand alone. They are long, difficult, and musically not important and I have not included any here since this collection is intended as a practical rather than historical anthology.

Liszt, the greatest all-round piano virtuoso who ever lived, unfortunately did not take up the challenge offered by left-hand writing. His only piece in the genre, an uncharacteristic transcription of one of his songs, was made for his friend and pupil, Count Geza Zichy, a gifted musician who early in life lost his right arm in a hunting accident. Zichy published a number of left-hand pieces. Many of his compositions and transcriptions, which he performed in concert (he was independently wealthy and only played for charities), seem to have remained unpublished.

Alkan, always deeply interested in the innermost recesses of the piano's possibilities, devised the interesting scheme of writing a set of three etudes, one for left hand, one for right hand, and the famous perpetual motion in which *both* hands are required to play in unison. According to a photostat, which is in my possession, of the contract between Alkan and his editor Richault, these pieces were bought for publication in 1846. Judging from their style, I suspect they were written still earlier, i.e. before his first really significant work, the Grande Sonate Op. 33, which was published in 1849. They are not representative of the originality of Alkan's mature harmonies and melodic style, the first two being somewhat Italianate (an influence almost extinct in Alkan's ripe music). They were given the opus number 76, Alkan's last, presumably after his death. Although these three pieces do not, from a musical standpoint, exhibit the qualities for which Alkan deserves to be remembered, they *are* major curiosities of great technical utility. Unfortunately they are very long and I have been able to include only the one for the left hand. There is also another work by Alkan which combines *in one piece* an etude for right hand alone, an etude for left hand alone, and

then a uniting of both hands, thus giving us a three-in-one etude. I consider this Etude in A Flat Major Op. 35, No. 8 one of the most perfect studies ever written. It combines fascinating technical utility with great musical beauty. It can be found in my edition of *The Piano Music of Alkan* (G. Schirmer).

Eduard Marxsen, Brahms's teacher, was interested in the left hand and wrote numerous pieces for it, the Impromptu Op. 33 being called "Hommage è Dreyschock." Brahms seems to have taken over Marxsens's interest in left-hand technique. (In general, he was intrigued by the technical possibilities of the piano, as witness his 51 Exercises.) Although he wrote no *original* pieces for left hand, the left-hand parts of his compositions are unusually ingenious, and he made a number of transcriptions for the development of the left hand. His transcription of Bach's Violin Chaconne in d minor for left hand alone was apparently done for Clara Schumann when she injured her right hand. It seems to have been a hobby of Brahms to play Bach's unaccompanied violin and cello music on the piano with his left hand. Brahms did four other transcriptions for two hands, in which the left hand is the prime beneficiary. None of the Brahms transcriptions has been included in this album because they are readily available in several extant editions.

Felix Blumenfeld, pupil of Anton Rubinstein and teacher of Vladimir Horowitz, has, in his *A-flat Etude* for left hand alone, written one of the most euphonious and technically useful of all left-hand compositions. Undoubtedly, the best-known left-hand piece today is Scriabin's *Nocturne*. It, and its companion piece, the *Prelude,* seem to have been written when Scriabin, trying to emulate the technique of his classmate, the future great pianist, Josef Lhévinne, strained his right hand practicing Liszt's *Don Juan Fantasy.* Unlike some lazy pupils that all of us can think of, he did not allow this setback to keep his left hand inactive.

It is not commonly known that, at about the same time as he wrote the Prelude and Nocturne, Scriabin also devised *another* left-hand piece which unfortunately was never published—in all likelihood it was never even written down. It has been variously mentioned as being a "paraphrase on Strauss' *Wine, Women and Song,*" and as a composition "after the manner of Strauss." Scriabin played it numerous times. Each time it became more elaborate. During his tour in America in 1907 he played it once, in New York, with great success, and then seemingly never again. No trace of it has been found.

One of the most delightful of all etude writers (in his case this is not a contradiction in terms) and one who understands fingers and the piano, and who at the same time knows how to sugarcoat the technical pill with charming and piquant music, is Moskowski — a real master of the genre. Almost all of his two-hand etudes (and he wrote many) give equal attention to the grubby left hand. But he also wrote twelve valuable etudes for the left hand alone.

Now we come to the most prolific and important of all left-hand composers—Leopold Godowsky, who was a life-long champion of left-hand music, and who, strangely enough, at the age of sixty, suffered a heart attack which paralyzed his right hand. He made twenty-two transcriptions for left hand alone of the Etudes of Chopin. His theory was "If it is possible to assign to the left hand alone the work done usually by both hands simultaneously, what vistas are opened to future composers were this attainment to be extended to both hands!" The *Meditation* and *Elegie* herein included are part of a Left-Hand Album which the composer later elaborated into an album for two hands. It is most interesting to compare the two versions.

The Viennese pianist, Paul Wittgenstein, who lost his right arm in the First World War, was responsible for the creation of a large body of music for left hand through his courageous resolve to commission important contemporary composers to write left-hand works for him. Thus it was that pieces by Strauss, Korngold, Franz Schmidt and numerous other composers—above all, Ravel—came into being. Unfortunately, most of these compositions have remained unpublished.

Every author knows the anguish of finally going to press. One's best ideas usually seem to occur after the publication deadline. Although I am here serving in the role merely of compiler and editor, author's pangs nevertheless beset me. I have several times been on the verge of going to press with this album. At the last minute, I would hear of another left-hand piece that sounded interesting and would halt everything until I could track it down. But there comes a time when one has to take a stand and say: "No more." I have arrived at that point.

Space and copyright laws (composers have the bad habit of wanting to get paid for their work!) have necessarily placed certain strictures on my choice of pieces for inclusion. And some works which might prove interesting have been to date, despite grueling search, unfindable. The search will continue, I assure you. If you find this collection as functional as I hope you will, perhaps it may be possible to give you an additional volume later.

THE EDUCATION OF THE LEFT HAND

The ambitious student, on discovering inadequacies in his left hand, will want to practice all the difficult passages he can lay his hands on. In fact, he will make it his business as a regular part of his practicing to go over, with his left hand, the *right-hand* parts of every piece he studies, *and* vice versa. Nothing is better for expanding the technique than playing things not conceived for the instrument, or which were written for the opposite hand. Liszt vastly stretched the technique of the pianist by adapting violin and orchestral music to the piano. And it is not generally realized that Chopin — most pianistic of all composers — developed his idiom of widespread chords, arpeggios, and figurations from violin technique.

Playing any given passage with the opposite hand can prove vastly stimulating. It is not simply a question of making one hand do what the other does, for the distribution of fingers is topsy-turvy, and the case would never be parallel unless the actual note patterns were inverted. Even then, to present really indentical problems to the fingers, passages must be inverted in a way that achieves the same distribution of black and white keys which exists in the original. Adolph Henselt in his *Exercises Préparatoires* gives numerous examples of *symmetric inversions*. One exercise, based on a left-hand passage from Chopin's *Etude Op. 25, No. 11*, will suffice to show you what I am talking about:

Attempts have been made to construct symmetrical inversions of entire Etudes of Chopin, but all this is very cumbersome and unnecessary.

A passage that may be easy for one hand, may be very awkward when played by the other hand—and consequently very rewarding to practice! Chopin and Liszt teem with passages where the left hand plays figurations either in unison with the right, or independently—figurations which are germane to right-hand technique. This style of writing offers special difficulty to the left hand.

It is very important for the person who wishes to develop his left-hand technique to have at hand a large amount of reading material for the left hand. Activity is the main thing. From that standpoint the pieces in this book can serve him well. Another very important source of reading material is violin or cello music—played on the piano with the left hand. The Bach sonatas and suites for violin, and for cello, are extremely good for this purpose, as are the Paganini caprices. I might also suggest that the really ambitious player should play *with his left hand* the *violin or cello part* of sonatas along with a gramophone recording. This will give him invaluable experience in sight-reading up to tempo and will prove most stimulating in every way. The same can be done with string concerti, with woodwind music, and so on. This also helps to develop familiarity with music other than that written strictly for the piano. A similar thing could be done on two pianos, with one pianist playing the piano part of any kind of instrumental duo which includes piano, while the left-hand specialist plays the other instrument's part with his left hand at the second piano.

The Contrapuntal Age by its very nature required equal development of each hand; but even then, there was a factor that seems to have run contrary to the development and maintenance of left-hand agility, for we find C.P.E. Bach, in his *Versuch über die wahre Art das Clavier zu spielen*, railing against the deleterious effects on the left hand of *continuo* playing (accompaniment from a figured bass) because of its tendency to stiffen the muscles by continued playing of octaves with the left hand. One wonders what he would have thought of Chopin's *A-flat Polonaise* or Liszt's *Funerailles* with their famous left-hand octave passages! It is still true, I think, even today, that the normal pianistic functions of the left hand, and the types of accompaniment it usually plays, militate against a good coloratura technique. That might be all well and good were it not for the fact that the piano literature contains famous passages where the left hand is expected to purl and twitter and glitter equally as well as the right hand. Therefore, the left hand must not only work hard to develop this ability, but must work to maintain it while its normal functions as accompanist often tend to destroy it. It goes without saying that diligent practice of Bach is bound to have beneficial effect on the left hand (and on most other aspects of your piano playing, musicianship, mind and soul). But Bach alone will not suffice to give the left hand the technique to encompass the difficult passages written for it by later composers. The left hand in Chopin, Liszt, Scriabin, and Rachmaninoff is often called upon to play *accompanying* figures of great complexity. These figures, by the way, have nothing to do with right-hand technique, and the right hand is seldom expected to do similar things. The *right hand* can profit vastly from practicing left-hand passages.

But it must be said that along with playing non-piano music and Bach, and music for opposite hands, it is very important to practice pieces *specifically* written for the *left hand* and to bring them up to performance level. For one profits most through repeated *finished performances* of a given composition. It is a current disease amongst teachers and students to begin pieces and then drop them long before they have been polished — this is euphemistically called "Putting them to soak." Unfortunately, they are seldom ever taken *out* of soak again! Great care should be exercised in choosing compositions which will not be too far beyond the student after a certain period of dedicated work. In today's pedagogical jargon a favorite term for living beyond one's pianistic means is "stretching piece." This usually amounts to being a piece preposterously difficult at the student's present level and one which he can't possibly play adequately. A pianist is not a giraffe. A piece that is too difficult to be vanquished within a reasonable period of time should not be taken up in the first place. It is only frustrating and injurious to the morale and technique of the player. However, many pieces which are dropped are dropped not because the pupil is incapable eventually of bringing them to the boil; rather, they are dropped because the pupil (and/or his teacher) does not know *how to practice* them to get them to performance level. This *is* a preface, not a treatise on practicing the piano, so I cannot go into great detail on the matter. However, I *shall* try to provide a number of methods and means for conquering the special and fascinating difficulties posed by left-hand playing.

THE PRACTICE AND PERFORMANCE OF ONE-HAND PIECES

The action of a modern grand piano becomes progressively heavier as one descends to the left end of the keyboard. A frequent fault in piano instruction is, indiscriminately, to tell the student to practice "slow and loud." As a matter of fact, loud practicing can be injurious to a young or weak hand. It can tend to tighten and cramp the hand and make it sluggish, just as the quest for power in singing can be injurious to the flexibility of the voice. *Speed and agility must be acquired first, and power only very gradually added.* The great harpsichord composer, Couperin, advised young pupils to practice on a lightly quilled harpsichord (i.e. one with a light action). The action of any harpsichord is considerably lighter than that of the modern grand piano, so one can imagine what Couperin would have thought of our pianos. One reason why the left hand is generally lacking in sufficient mobility is that it plays in an area which requires more force than the right hand. It is true, also, that in the piano's nether regions the left hand can make more noise than the right hand playing in more celestial precincts. Many teachers assign their pupils pieces such as the so-called *Revolutionary Etude* of Chopin to improve their left hands. This is precisely the sort of piece which should *not* be assigned to pupils who do not already have a very considerable practice and mastery in playing scale and arpeggio patterns of the simpler kind, because the patterns used by Chopin are sophisticated and widespread over the keyboard, requiring great stretches and

very adroit passage of thumb under fingers and fingers over thumb in awkward positions and at the same time demanding great strength. The unschooled hand attacking such a work will squirm around and do itself more harm than good, besides murdering a masterpiece. No — cultivation of mobility and speed, with rhythmical precision, definitely must precede acquisition of force. Furthermore, a piece such as the *Revolutionary Etude* is too easily fakeable; that is to say, temperament and display of force can lull the unfastidious ear of the inexperienced player or listener into thinking that he is hearing the real thing. The fact is, one learns most about technique from passionless finger pieces. Therefore, Czerny (brought up to performance level) can often be, for the neophyte's fingers, much more healthful than Chopin.

Separate Hands Practice

Many of the great works of the piano literature contain passages for the left hand which are as difficult as anything that the right hand is required to play. So the poor left hand, which has been in subservient position supplying accompaniments or oom-pah-pahs, is suddenly called out of the pantry and expected to appear as the belle of the ball. I feel very strongly that students should do a great deal of hands-separate practicing, because only then can they hear really well what the fingers are up to. All two-hand pieces should be practiced left hand alone first until you are very certain of your left hand's ability (few pianists have reason to be) and until the part is *mastered* and *memorized*. Difficult accompaniment passages such as are to be found frequently in Chopin (for instance, *Nocturne in e minor)* should be practiced assiduously, *left hand alone,* making all the crossing-over (and *under*) connections with scrupulous attention to *legato* and without relying on the pedal to simulate a *legato*. The oom-pah-pah accompaniments of Chopin waltzes require very special attention and care, and should be practiced left hand alone until thoroughly mastered, and *before* starting to practice the right hand. As a matter of fact, anyone starting out to learn his first Chopin waltz should first read through the *entire* book left hand alone numerous times, taking great care to observe the rule of thumb (or rather, 5th finger) that all "oom" notes (first beats) should be played with the *5th finger* and that the 5th should not be employed in the "pah-pahs" (2nd and 3rd beats) unless the stretches are such that the 5th *must* be employed. Naturally, care is going to have to be taken, when putting the hands together, that the left hand does not over-balance the right hand. Remember always that it is usually easy for the left hand to drown out the right hand, and it is an unfair and ignoble victory. Prima donnas of the last century used to have a clause in their contracts exempting them from attending operatic rehearsals. Do not allow your prima donna right hand any such privileges. Right hand alone practice can be very revealing and should be indulged in *frequently*. You cannot afford to leave any corner of your pianism unattended for too long. Dust settles in with alarming rapidity, and if the upstairs maid (you) is lax, she'll find her parlor festooned with cobwebs, even down to her prized right hand.

I have just advised you to practice hands separately in all of your two-hand pieces. I now want to advise you to do precisely the same thing in all your *one-hand* pieces. Before you hasten to a conclusion about my mental health let me point out that most pieces written for the left hand really do have parts for two hands; that is to say, they have accompanying figures which are, so to speak, for the left hand, and a melody which is, so to speak, for the right hand; and the pedal holds sounds for you in widely dispersed areas of the keyboard making everything plausible to the ear. Therefore, when I advise you to practice one-hand pieces hands separately, what I mean is that, in a piece such as the Chopin-Godowsky *E-flat minor etude,* you would—in particularly difficult places—omit the melody and practice the figuration first, always, of course, playing in strict time and leaving rests where the melody ordinarily would be.

The Two Basic Types of One-Hand Pieces

1. *Monodic* — Single-note passage work implying its own bass and harmony, such as in the Saint-Saëns *Moto Perpetuo*. It is unfortunate that this type of left hand composition is definitely in the minority because such pieces are highly beneficial to the player as an aid to evening out the bumps in his technique by cultivating smooth passing-under of the thumb and the passing of other fingers over the thumb. It is precisely this sort of thing that is most required of the left hand in difficult passages in *two-hand* music. I would advise students to make and perform transcriptions from the running movements in Bach's violin and cello sonatas, partitas, suites, etc.

There are a very few *two-hand pieces* which fit into this category—in which both hands play the same notes an octave or two octaves apart. The greatest unison *perpetuo mobile* ever written for the piano is undoubtedly the finale of Chopin's *B-flat minor Sonata*. The technical value of this piece (aside from its supreme musical originality) is immense. A starter piece with similar technical problems *en miniature* is Chopin's *E-flat minor Prelude,* although the character of that work is quite different, being heavy and much slower. The only other work of this nature technically worthy, though not musically, of being mentioned in the same breath as these two pieces is Alkan's *Perpetual Motion.* In some ways, this composition is even more difficult than the Chopin finale, because it is much longer and requires great endurance. It also contains lengthy passages with very wide stretches. With the exception of these passages, the figurations are of the older Beethoven-Weber-Czerny type which really should be mastered before going on to the infinitely more subtle convolutions of Chopin's passage work. It goes without saying that the left-hand part of these pieces should be thoroughly learned and practiced before the right hand is taken up, and I see no objection to playing *alone* the left hand part of these works at student recitals (though not at public concerts) as left-hand challenges. The right hand should deign to practice its part diligently, alone, when the time comes, and it should be worked up to the ultimate tempo of which *it* is capable—which will no doubt be faster than what the left hand can achieve. When the time comes to practice both hands together, I prescribe large doses of practice *with the hands crossed* — left hand *over* right, and then left hand *under* right both one and two octaves apart—a great test of coordination. When this handicap is removed and the hands are played in normal position life will suddenly seem much rosier. This method of practice can be applied very profitably to all unison passages and to five-finger exercises such as Hanon.

ATTENTION. When you first try this, have someone standing by to untangle you, or you may expire from suffocation.

2. *Contrapuntal* — By far the most frequent type of left-hand piece is the kind in which the left hand is, with the aid of the pedal, made to sound like two hands by performing the function of playing a melody, a bass-line, and an accompaniment which frequently entwines contrapuntally around the melody. These various elements have to be kept on different dynamic planes, melody predominating, bass-line next in importance, and accompaniment most subdued. (See my comments above about "separate hand" practice of one-hand pieces.)

Fingering of One-Hand Pieces

The fingering of pieces for left hand alone is of immense importance. Many times, very special and seemingly unorthodox fingerings will have to be used. It is difficult to lay down rules for adequate fingering of left-hand pieces, or two-hand pieces, for that matter. The best way to learn how to find serviceable fingering is through examining and comparing the fingerings in many, many pieces as marked by composers and qualified editors, and by not being too hasty in rejecting their fingering until you are certain that yours is better. It will take experience to *know* whether yours is better. What may be feasible at a slow tempo before the piece is learned may not be at all practicable at proper tempo. Godowsky's fingerings, in his pieces both for one and two hands, are models of subtlety and exquisite refinement—incredibly ingenious—and should be scrutinized with special assiduity for they can open up new horizons in the player's approach to piano playing. Godowsky had a small hand but it was made of rubber and he employs all manner of unexpected and fascinating stretches between the fingers, as you will see if you take the trouble to practice his fastidious fingerings. These fingerings, with all their exotic twistings and turnings, passings under and over, and silent substitutions, are a sensual pleasure to the hands—which will begin to feel boneless and maleable as putty after you study a few of Godowsky's works.

In the present collection it has been my policy always to use the composer's fingerings when they have been supplied and to add nothing to them. Max Reger states in his Etudes that he feels the player should find his own fingerings and I have respected his wishes by giving none. Coincidentally, Debussy in his set of Etudes for two hands was of the same opinion. In one way I agree with Reger and Debussy. Still, one would be very interested to have their personal fingerings which could not help being instructive. I have supplied some fingerings for the Scriabin pieces and the Blumenfeld *Etude* since these composers apparently published the pieces without fingerings, but they did not specifically stipulate that the player should find his own. My fingerings for these pieces will give an idea of my opinions about fingerings. The player, if he likes them, can deduce formulas from them to be applied to other pieces which I have left bare.

One rule that I can insist upon categorically for artistic reasons, is to avoid, unless absolutely necessary because of a small hand, the favorite trick of placing the thumb simultaneously on two adjacent keys. In left-hand music, the top note is usually the melodic note, and if the thumb is playing *two* keys the player is unable to bring out the upper melody tone, except by an extreme amount of dexterity and experience. As a matter of fact, in really sensitive piano playing that sort of fingering should be avoided in either hand as much as possible because it does not allow for a true contrapuntal treatment and balancing of chords.

The thumb, because of its strength and broad playing surface, is capable of drawing out of the piano an immense quantity of sound, and a sound that is fuller and richer and more certain of aim than that produced by such well-known expedients as playing a note with the 2nd and 3rd fingers, or 3rd and 4th fingers clamped together. Therefore, make use of the thumb for high notes of phrases and notes requiring special emphasis (this applies, also, to the right hand). In rare cases, a particularly strong note can be played by the fifth finger side of the hand doubled up as a fist (black keys only) or by the fifth finger used flat on its side (white keys only).

Choice of fingering can depend on the way a note or group of notes is meant to sound. For instance, the following sort of note distribution, frequently found in left-hand music, can conceivably be fingered in any one of the following ways:

But if a strong full tone is desired on the upper note, the following "untraditional" fingering is the most secure:

(See my fingerings in the Scriabin pieces)

The above chord may, especially in a transcription of a string piece, sound best as follows:

Pedaling of One-Hand Pieces

Anton Rubinstein said that the pedal is the soul of the piano. Two-hand contrapuntal music is possible sometimes without the pedal. All of Bach's klavier music was written for instruments that had no sustaining pedal — though when we play that music on the piano the pedal is used for coloristic reasons. But *one-hand* pieces of the contrapuntal variety are simply unthinkable without the pedal. Here the foot becomes an extension of the fingers and it is needed constantly to hold on to sounds while the fingers move to other regions of the keyboard. Sometimes a bold pedaling is necessary, which may cause a blur or wash of sound that could be avoided if one were using two hands, but which, in one-hand

music is to be preferred to letting essential sounds, such as important bass notes, die before their time. It is often said that it is impossible to indicate pedalings — they depend on the piano, acoustics, etc. This is only partially true. There are always certain places which can *only* be pedaled correctly in one way. And this is infinitely truer in one-hand than two-hand music. Careful study of Godowsky's jeweler-precise pedaling indications can give you a basis for arriving at your own pedaling in other pieces.

The following example from Scriabin's *Nocturne* for left hand is usually pedaled as at B . But this obliterates the bass and tenor (F and A♭) and leaves the melody stranded in mid-air with no supporting harmony. I consider A to be the only possible realization of Scriabin's notation, which specifically asks to have the F and A♭ sustained throughout. Timid souls will object to the slight and unavoidable melodic blur. Too bad.

Deportment

In practicing and playing one-hand pieces, the non-playing hand must remain relaxed, *unclutched and unclutching.* Think of the ballet dancer who, while performing terribly exerting feats such as a series of sixteen *entre-chats huit,* wears a perpetual smile and keeps his arms as seemingly relaxed and disembodied as though he were executing a simple *plié,* and without showing the slightest sign of effort facially or elsewhere while jumping up into the scenery. In playing the piano, each part of the body must be isolated and be capable of functioning independently. However, in playing left-hand pieces one can occasionally support and steady oneself with the right hand by putting it on the edge of the bench and leaning on it while one plays in the upper register with the left hand. A bench will also allow you to shift your whole body gently an inch or so depending on which range of the keyboard you have to command. In general, in playing left-hand pieces you should sit a bit to the right of the center of the keyboard, rather than approximately in the center as for two-hand pieces.

I strongly recommend the use of a bench rather than a piano stool or chair for all piano playing, but especially for one-hand piano playing, because one is very easily thrown off balance while sitting on a chair or stool, and you may suddenly find yourself *not* sitting on a chair or stool (one of the occupational hazards of playing the piano). A painful "back-log" of personal experience prompts this warning.

CONTENTS

PIANO MUSIC FOR ONE HAND
Selected and Edited by RAYMOND LEWENTHAL

Gavotte in E

Transcribed for the left hand
by Rafael Joseffy

Johann Sebastian Bach

Joseffy's realizations of Bach's ornaments leaves something to be desired, but I nevertheless quote them exactly as he wrote them. There are also minor discrepancies in repetitions of phrases, but I have decided to let them stand as is (Editor's note).

Solfeggietto

Arranged for left hand
by A. R. Parsons

Carl Phil. Em. Bach

Non troppo vivo

Etude for the left hand

Ludwig Berger

(No. 9 from 12 Etudes for the Left Hand, Op. 12)

To Monsieur Léopold Godowsky

Etude
for the left hand alone

Felix Blumenfeld, Op. 36

The fingerings are the editors.

Pochissimo meno mosso
marcato sempre

Tempo I

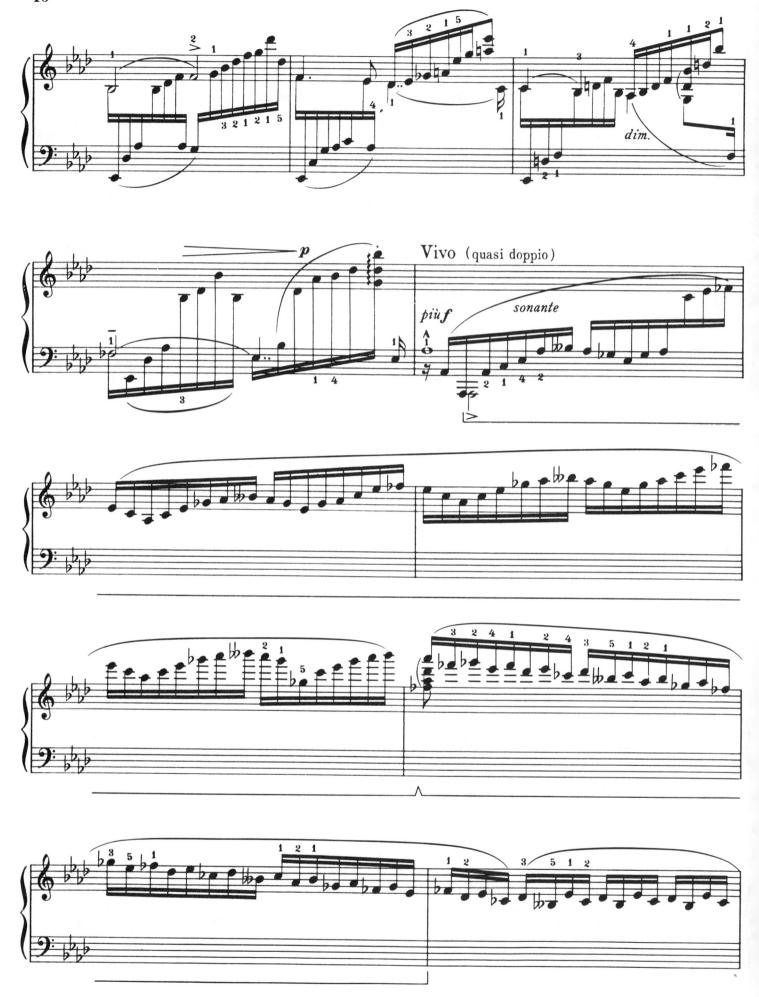

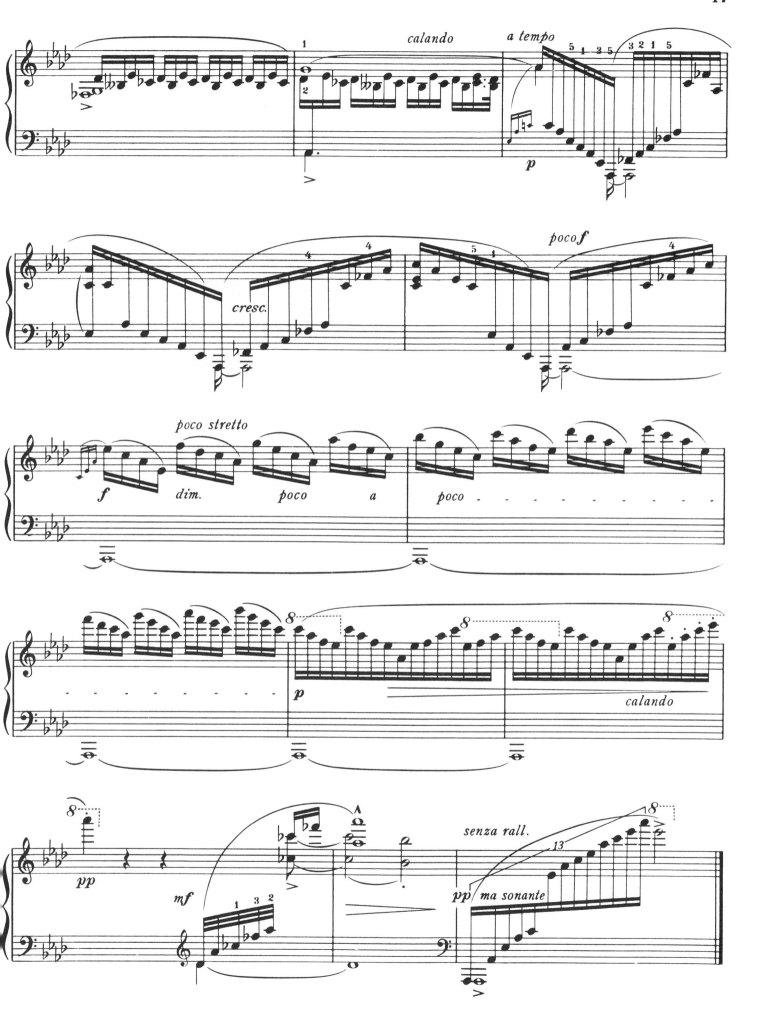

Four-Voiced Fugue
for left hand

Friedrich Kalkbrenner

Etude for One Hand

Revised and fingered
by Isidór Philipp

Carl Czerny

* This etude will be beneficial for each hand.   Fingering for the left hand is printed below the notes.   (I.P.)

22

La Ricordanza

Eduard Marxsen
(from 3 Impromptus Op.33 "Hommage a Dreyscheck")

Andante ma non troppo

Etude in E♭ minor

No. 3 from 22 Etudes of Chopin
Transcribed for the Left Hand Alone by Leopold Godowsky

Frédéric Chopin, Op. 10, No. 6

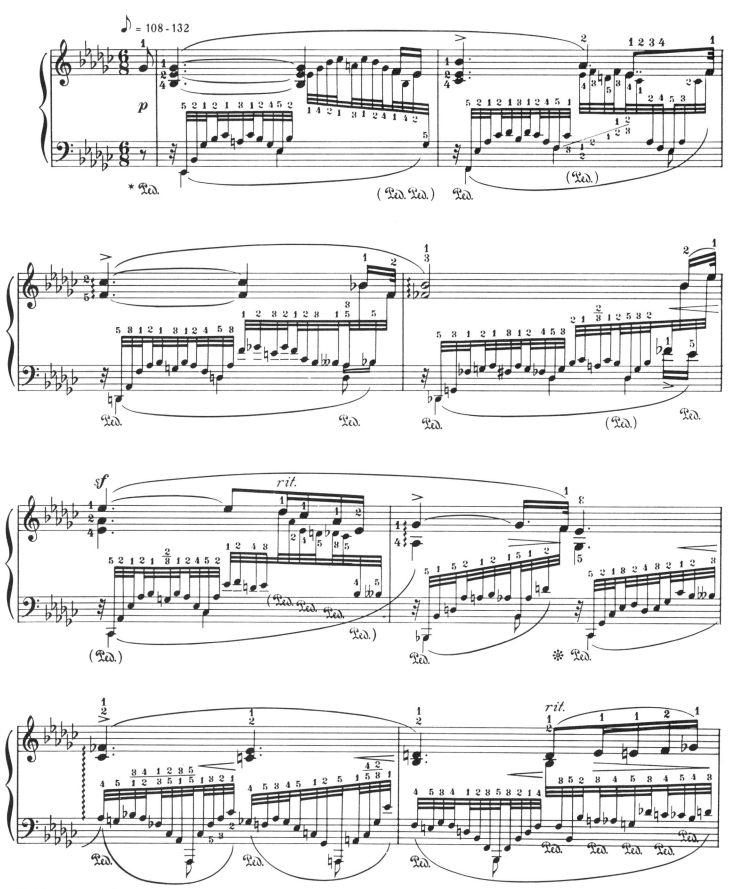

(Ped.) is Godowsky's way of marking optional changes of pedal. He was very precise in marking pedalings and fingerings and they should all be studied with great care, (Editor's note).

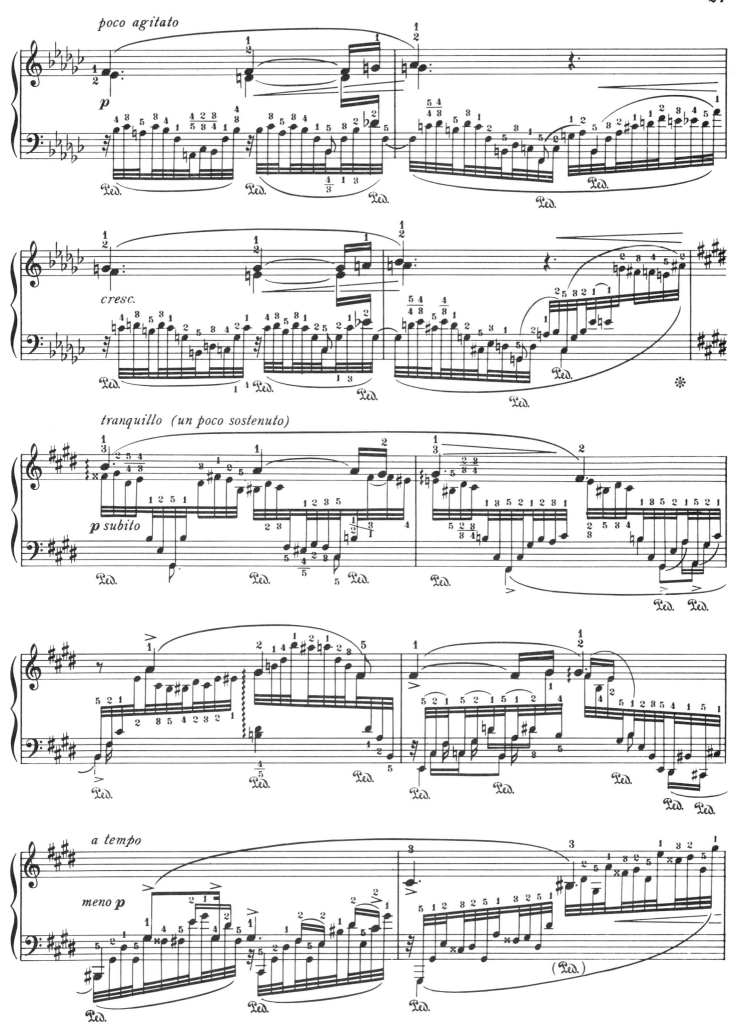

28

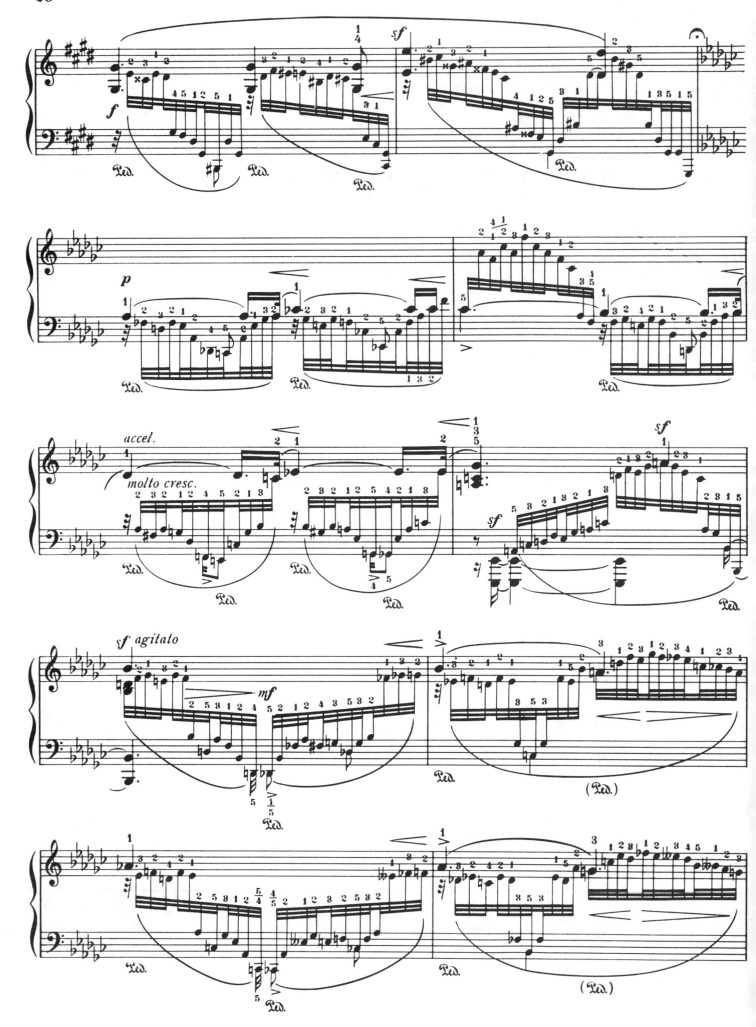

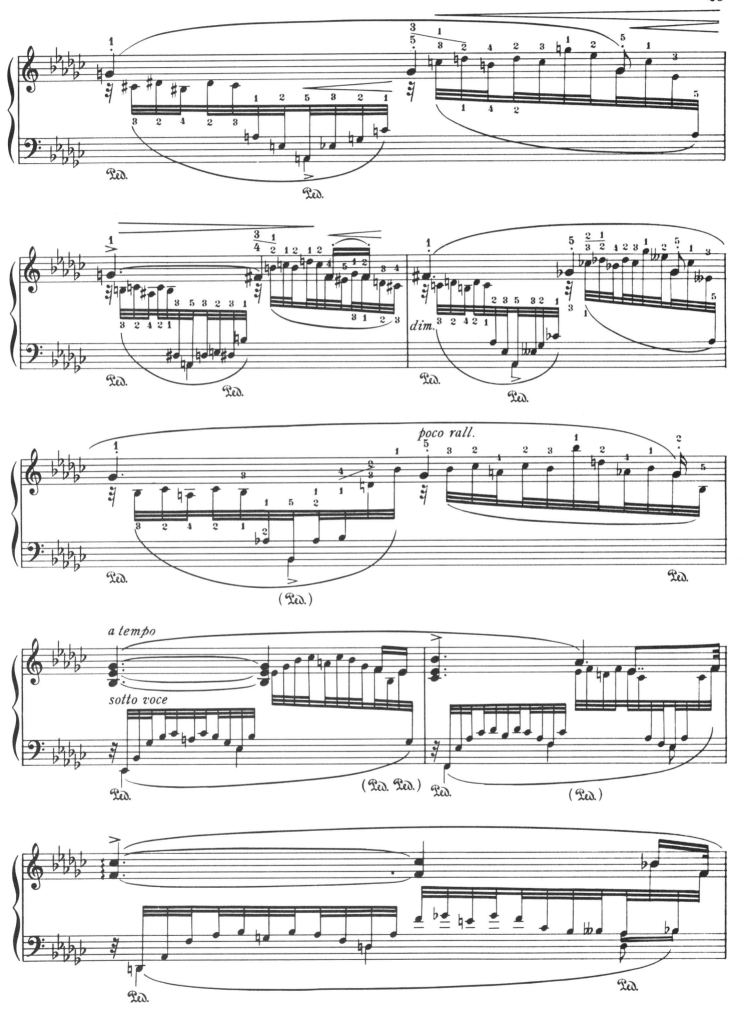

Hungary's God

After a poem by Alexander Petöfi

Franz Liszt

Animato

Fantasy in A♭

Charles Valentin Alkan
(No. 1 from Three Grand Etudes, Op. 76)

Largamente

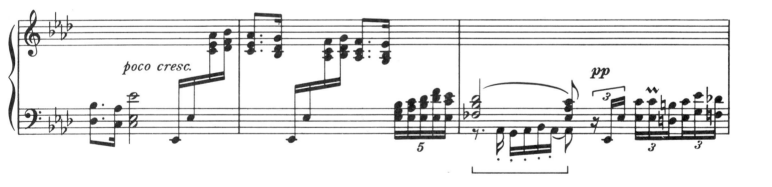

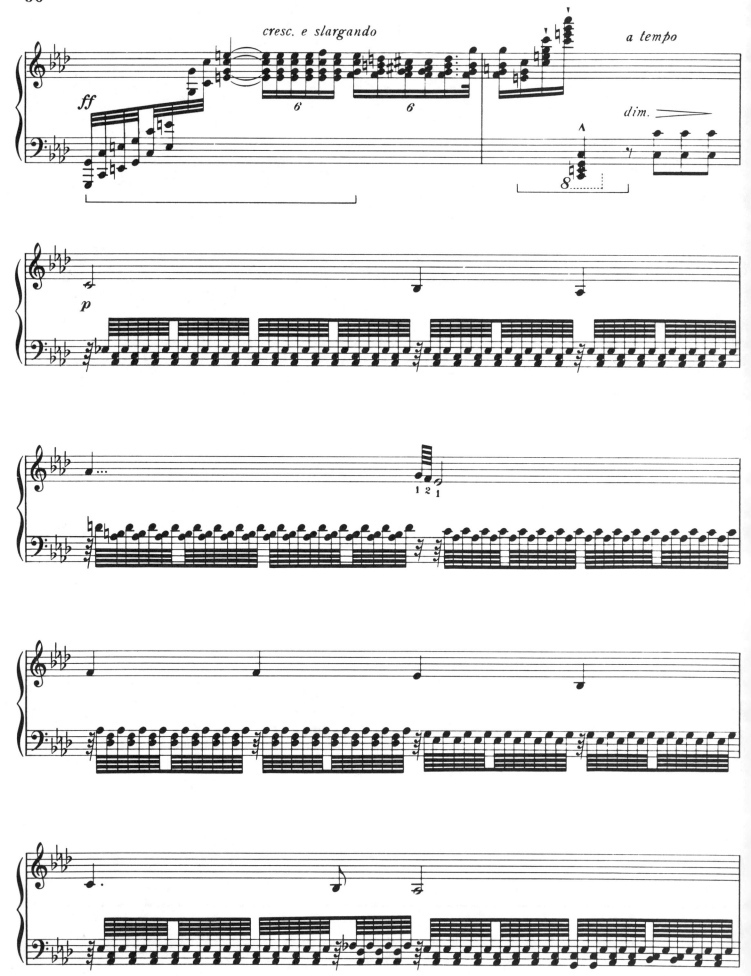

Allegro vivace

42

Gravemente

Three Folk Songs for the left hand

The melody must sound clearer than the accompaniment

Louis Köhler
(from School of the Left Hand, Op. 302)

Rhythmic Studies

Play each 16th note nearly as quick as a grace-note
Play each section five times

Louis Köhler
(from School of the Left Hand, Op. 302)

1

Allegretto moderato ♩ = 108

2

Allegretto ♩ = 96

Exercise in Arpeggio

Louis Köhler
(from School of the Left Hand, Op. 302)

Etude for the left hand

F. W. Greulich
(from Etudes de Salon, Op. 19)

Melody from Weber's Freischütz

for the left hand

Louis Köhler

(from School of the Left Hand, Op. 302)

Etude No. 3

F. Bonimici

(No. 3 from 34 Melodious Etudes for the Left Hand Alone, Op. 273)

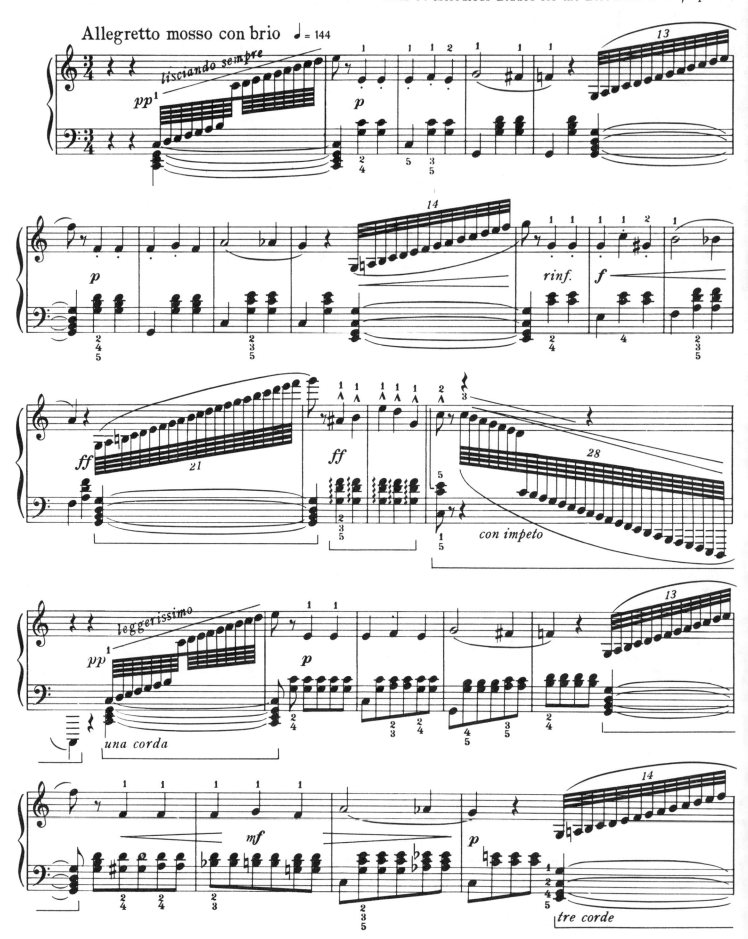

The glissandi should be played strictly in time and careful attention should be payed as to whether they get one or two beats (Editor's note).

58

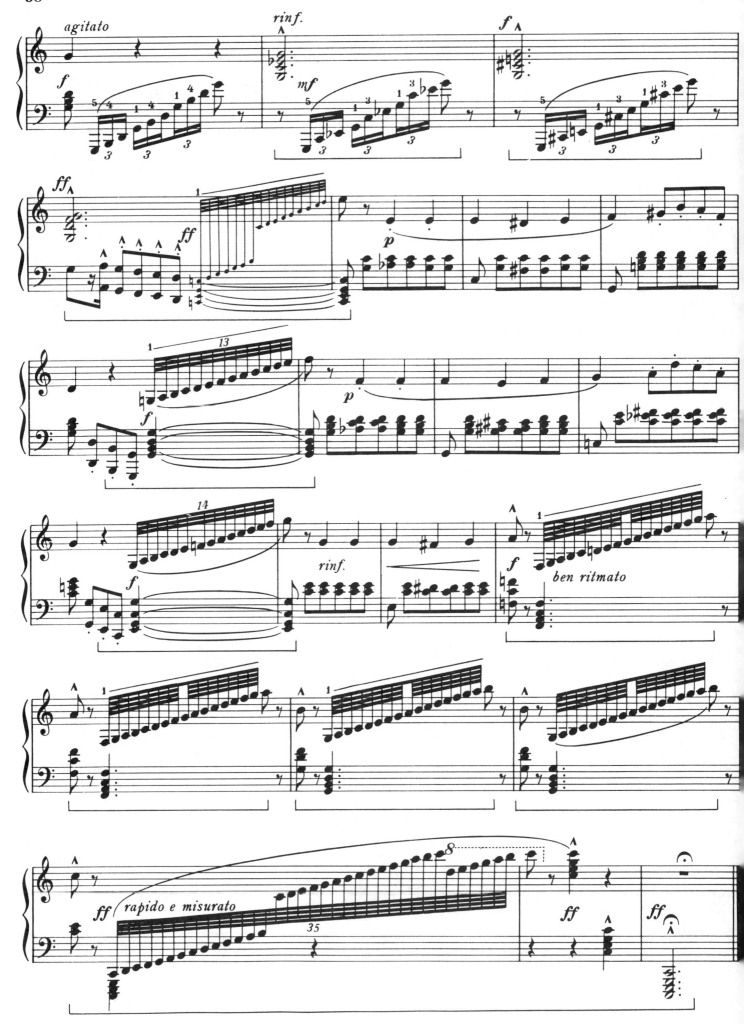

Finale

Carl Reinecke
(from Sonata for the Left Hand, Op.179)

64

9 Etudes
from: The Training of the left hand (25 Studies)

No. 4

Hermann Berens
(from The Training of the Left Hand, Op. 89)

Allegro risoluto
marcato

No. 9

Moderato cantabile
con espressione

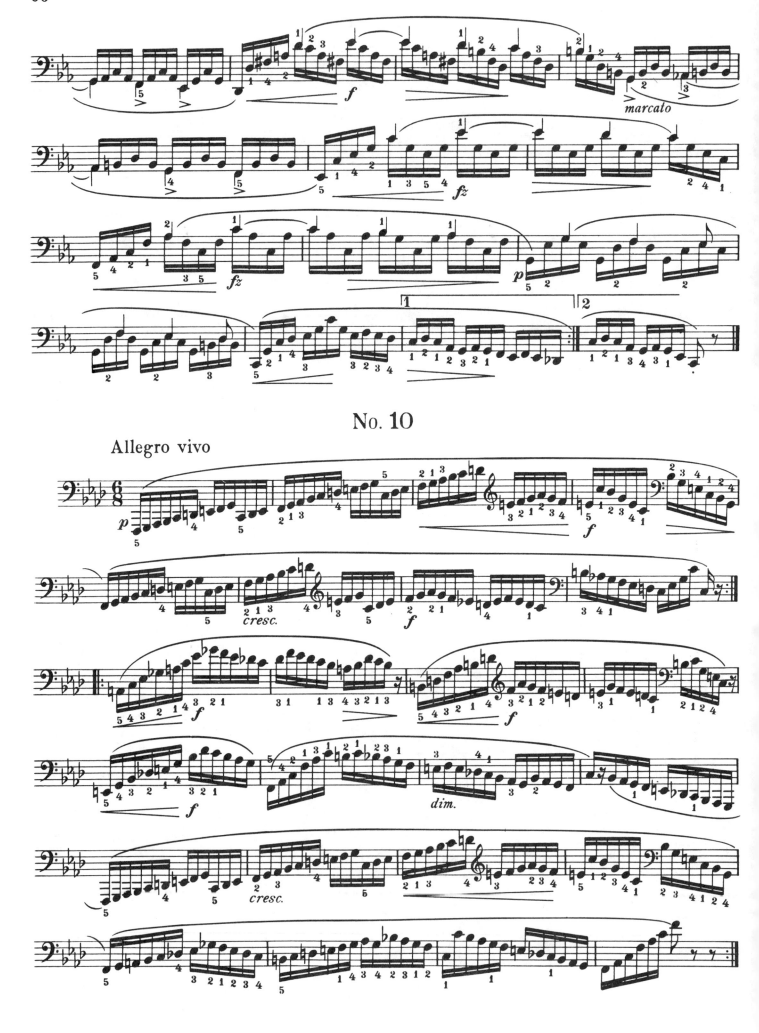

No. 10

Allegro vivo

No. 11

Chorale
Andante

No. 12

Allegro

No. 13

Allegro moderato

Allegro risoluto

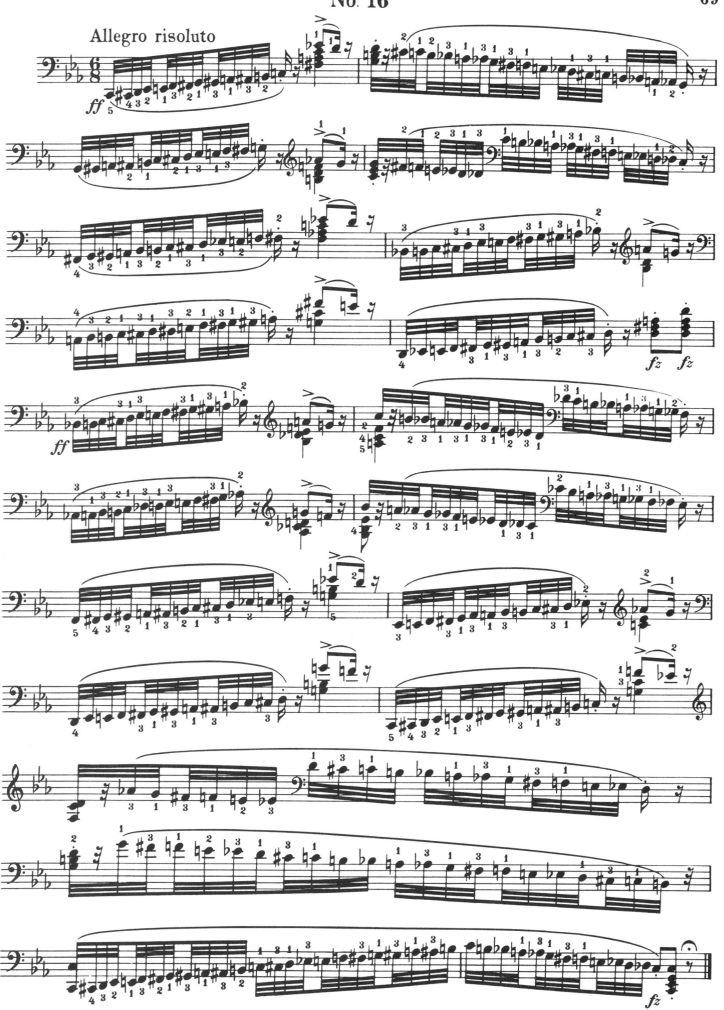

No. 18

Allegro con fuoco

No. 23

Andante espressivo

Exercise

The first note of every measure lightly arpeggiated

Wilhelm Tappert
(No. 22 from 48 Exercises for the Left Hand)

Exercise

Wilhelm Tappert
No. 45 from 48 Exercises for the Left Hand)

* H means $\begin{smallmatrix}1\\2\\3\\4\\5\end{smallmatrix}$, to be used by large hands. Alternative fingering for large hands are printed above some chords (Composer's note).

Moto Perpetuo

Camille Saint Saëns
(No. 3 from Six Etudes for the Left Hand, Op. 135)

Allegretto   Doux et tranquille - sans vitesse et très également
(Gentle and tranquil, not fast and very evenly)

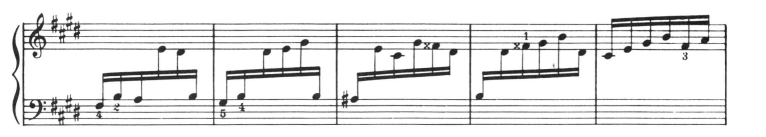

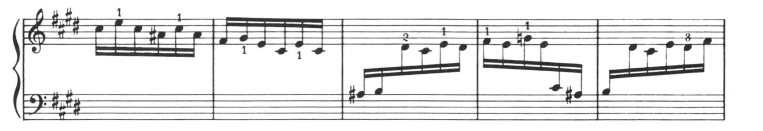

poco cresc.

mf

Viennese Pranks

Géza Zichy
(No. 4 from 4 Etudes for the Left Hand alone)

To Harold Bauer

Etude

Moritz Moszkowski
(No. 4 from 12 Etudes for the Left Hand alone, Op. 92)

Meditation

Leopold Godowsky
(No. 1 from Concert Album for the Left Hand alone)

* The arpeggio should be played leisurely as an up-beat to the top G. The melody must float above all other voices.

(Composer's note)

* A faster trill is admissible (Composer's note).

88

* With the lower octave (E♭), if desired (Composer's note).

Paris, France, January 23ʳᵈ 1929

Elegy

Leopold Godowsky
(No. 5 from Concert Album for the Left Hand alone)

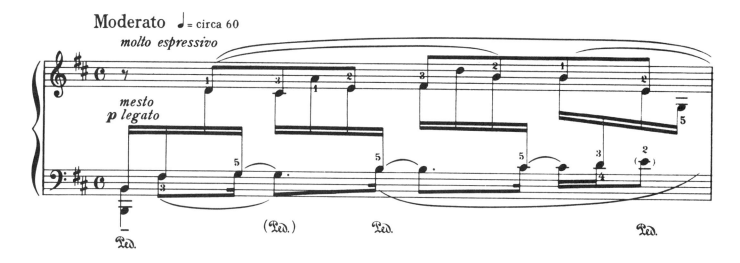

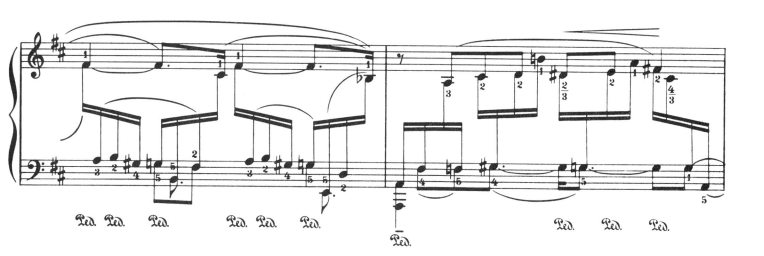

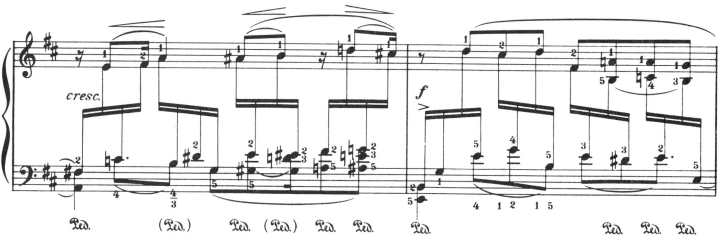

For Pedal note, see page viii

Paris, France, March 6, 1929

Prelude
for the left hand

Alexander Scriabin, Op. 9, No. 1

Andante

Fingerings in this piece are by the editor

94

Nocturne
for the left hand

Alexander Scriabin, Op. 9, No. 2
(1894)

*See page VIII in Preface, regarding pedaling (Editor's note).
Fingerings and pedalings in this piece are by the editor.

* Note the rhythm which is confusing to the eye as Scriabin has written it (Editor's note).

** A thorough study of the two clever cadenzas in this piece can bring your left hand a very long way technically. Do not consider it beyond you to devote the better part of several consecutive days to doing these exercises many many times. They can only do you good. They, and the original cadenza, should also be transposed to *all keys*, same fingerings (Editor's note).

* I believe this should be a trill between E♮ and F♮. Some pianists play F♯ which sounds wrong to me (Editor's note).

Four Special Studies
for the left hand alone

1
Scherzo

Max Reger

I purposely have not indicated fingering, as I deem it important for the player to find his own (Composer's note).

2
Humoreske

3
Romanze

Andante espressivo

4
Prelude and Fugue

To Lester Donahue

Capriccio in E flat
for the right hand

Rudolph Ganz, Op. 26, No. 2

Allegro moderato (Tempo di Gavotta)

*) Release sustaining Pedal

114

*) Release sustaining Pedal

Etude for the left hand

Béla Bartók
(Budapest, 1903)

46502

* I quote this rhythm as it appears in the original edition. It is obviously wrong. It probably should read ♩♪♪

(Editor's note).

Klavierstück

for the right or left hand alone

Carl Phil. Em. Bach